Life on Earth
POEMS

Stephen "Esteban" Lewis

DORRANCE PUBLISHING CO
EST. 1920
PITTSBURGH, PENNSYLVANIA 15238

Dorrance Publishing Co
585 Alpha Drive
Suite 103
Pittsburgh, PA 15238
Visit our website at *www.dorrancebookstore.com*

ISBN: 978-1-6376-4161-3
eISBN: 978-1-6376-4798-1

Life on Earth
POEMS

TREES

Trees make the scene.
They sway and wave while they're green
Cool it down on a hot sunny day
Fruit on the limb, summer days
Old oaks are best with horizontal trunks.
You can build a box in some
Fun to climb, swing on a limb.
But don't climb a Chinaberry tree,
They are very brittle.
If you do you'll find yourself saying,
"Really?" as you plummet
With snapped branch in hand.

MARTENEMER

I got a new pair of shoes
They're loafers with tassels on the front
A great fit, spaced just enough
They have a metal tag
Secured with brads
To the back of the sole
And reads genuine snakeskin
They're light as leaves
And I think mostly leather
I asked a dapper man
What would go well with shoes
Blue jeans and a white shirt
The shirt has to be white, he said
That sounded right
I put them on and did a stroll
They looked good, I was told
They're blue
That ok with you

HELP SPIDERS

Spiders HELP or
HELP spiders or
HELP, there's a Brown Recluse
In the bathtub
Worse yet, HELP, there's a Brown Recluse
On me.
Even more serious, HELP, there's a Brown Recluse
And a Black Widow spider fighting
Near me.
Then there's HELP, I see three Wolf spiders
Inside. Ran outside
Only to be confronted by a tarantula
Poised to jump up and bite me
On the face
With its green fangs
But I wouldn't kill it
Or any spider ever.

GOD

Heed me, please.
Hear my plea.
I am way awake
So concise with views
And serious plans
You'll arc to me.
I know you see too;
Strengthen your vessel, me.
I'll still tell promises to forget
But don't off me just yet!
And let me stay; (oops)
Let me stay, please,
On this crust
To do my earthly musts
While I am less than
One forever fading dot
In your creation.

HOUSE

A house that's roomy enough
Spent days and days
Putting stuff in the house and later
Months and months
Getting stuff out of the house
To me its harder taking stuff out of a house
Than putting stuff in ONE
Because a coffee table is still living in the garage.
The one you don't use
Tomorrow you say it's going to the refuse
So you thought and you know it becomes a no-way
Not tomorrow. Maybe the next day
So you say again.

REGRETS

Don't think it now
It can scar your mind
Think it right next time.

COMIC BOOKS

These heroes are brutal.
They fight really good.
They're macho bad ass
And slice off your head.
They fly and run fast and breathe under water;
Swordsmen to gods,
Archers and surfers
They come from all worlds
And there are many.
They all fight evil
And never need money
Except for Spiderman.

THE FLOOR

A dirty carpet covered the floor.
I ripped it out wall to door,
Rolled it up and hauled it away.
I'll cover this slab another day.
Yay!! No more stuck dirt and cat wizz.
Later a stained floor I'd miss
So a mahogany red I chose for the color.
It turned out okay and like no other.
Cooler in the winter and cool in the summer.
Later I'll spring for some slats.
I'll get them soon so there's a spring in my step
And not break my back.

HOMEGROWN TOMATOES

Tomatoes are good
To grow on your own.
To get ripe and red on the plant;
Great for BLTs and salads too.
They are green on the vine
And before you know it
Turning pink, orange, then red.
They are juicy. Yes,
Firm and nice to slice,
Share with neighbors
And preserve if the weather's nice.
It's a hobby and exercise
But lots of work
Mostly in the spring
And if it's pouring rain too much
You need to get a greenhouse.

LIFE

Instant gratification
Could be laziness
Obtaining it procrastination
A thousand weak reasons
To deter starting new.
A strong one to start
That's in your head too.
Get a bad one out, progression.
Nine hundred ninety-nine more to do

ARTWORK AND A WORK OF ART

I have a carving of a bird on a limb.
Its sharp beak and crested red head
Clearly marks him
It can hang up and down,
Sideways or upside down;
It doesn't matter
Sound deep in the woods a distant jackhammer
And some wonder do they get headaches
These woodpeckers are a piece of work
And a work of art
It was made in Mexico.

STICKS AND STONES

Sticks and stones can break your bones
Try not to let bad words hurt you
If you heed too long
It'll cramp you down
When people yell and try to slow you
Don't let it bother
Let it go out the other
Don't even listen unless it's
Watch. Look out.
Be careful. Fire. And others
Like run for your life.
Here's a twenty.
Heads up. It's a bomb, get away
Or get to a tree
There's a ten-pack of skinny
Gleam-toothed hyenas
With the slobbers
Pounding the corner, then straight
Sprinting fast, headed your way.

DUST

Dust, Dust is in the house
It's always there and can't be stopped
All over the chair and on the couch
On the table, desks, and shelves
A damp cloth does help.
They say dust is dead skin flakes
From humans mostly
The rest is dirt and dander, to me amazing
It's on the clock in every house
It's on the bed, covers the sheets.
Way up in the attic it sits.
It's on the stand under the bed.
Surrounding the floor and
If you don't use carpet you see lots more
On your fixtures and utensils
Don't forget the doors.
HOLD IT, HOLD IT, Wait up a sec.
Human skin flakes in the attic!!!
Nobody lives up there
Run for your life
And get out of the house now, kinfolk!
And call the Po Po!

OLD ZOOS

Cheetahs no quarter-mile dash
Polar bears no berg to raft
Alligators fat in the water
Giraffes no taller
Elephant no matriarch march
Kangaroos must walk
Hogs no dig to hide
Lion no hog to maul
Monkeys no screaming flight
Zebras just black 'n white.
Leopard no stealth
Koalas stare
Parrot no pristine
Deer no spring
Ostrich no plume up
Fox gave up
Frog no bright poison
Crocs no dinner roll.
All pace in their cages.
Zoos the cage
People stare
Lock the gate
Collect the fare
Gut a chicken
Scrub the walls
Sweep the shit
And dump the compost
That takes two
Me no like the old zoos.

COOL RALPH THE DOG

Ralph is a dog
Who sits on a log
In the morning fog.
If he sees a hog
He'll pursue with a jog
With his tongue hanging out
While panting with spit slinging about.
They do that to cool down
When they get too hot
Unlike humans, who sweat a lot
When they get hot.
So your pet that runs a lot
Will need to vent or see a vet
Because dogs cannot so do not sweat
Like humans do to keep cool.

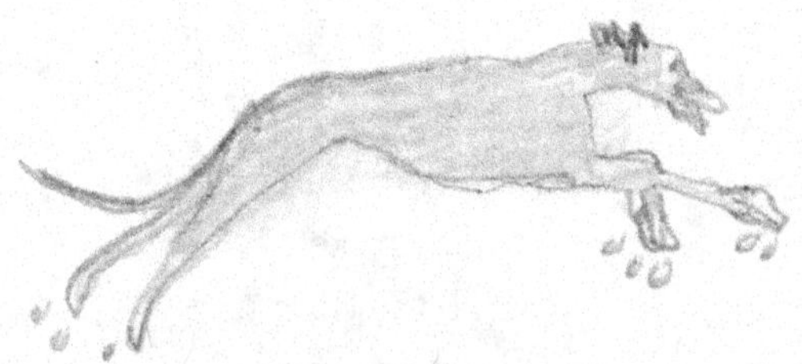

TRAFFIC

Wheeling down the road,
Running smooth, you're feeling it
Driven for years, it's automatic
You get to where there's too many cars.
You approach a turnpike, waiting to merge
It's hard to get there. You're in a new burg.
Glance to the back and to the sides.
Gauge the best time to make your slide.
Balk and brake, glitching the flow,
Got to stay on track. How will you know?
Click in a disc. Turn up the tunes.
Music's here to clear up the fumes.
Music can make driving a breeze.
Thank you, Muddy Waters
For making driving a breeze.

BRUSSELS SPROUTS

Like baby devil cabbages
Quadruple concentrated yuck
I gag before I can bite one
They're too rich for me
Lots of good stuff in them
Round, powerful, and green
Steaming and reeking
They assault my senses
I see them. I go around
I'm not fond of Brussels sprouts

SUMMERTIME IS THE BEST

Hot and muggy
Lots of bugs
Gnats and mosquitoes
Head to toe
To suck your blood, make you sick.
Get the repellant, make it stick.
Sun will burn you, make you bubble.
Use the sunscreen. Your skin's in trouble.
Cry for rain! It's a hot one, humid too!
When it comes it's too wet, turbid too.
Poison ivy makes you scratch
Just like oak and poison sumac.
Swirling winds sling grass and pollen
To stop your nose, clog your throat and brain.
Arghh! Now look, I can't breathe or talk, you complain.
But birds are talking and
You can watch them dance.
They mind their action
To their perfect best.
Soaring hawk, languid speck in the sky,
Suddenly plummet, dropped by a cloud spearing its way,
To rake a low-down grouse in flight.
Near miles of height, I awe their sight
Watching birds is for all seasons.
You have your season reasons.
Summertime is the best to me.
Enduring summers walls is but for the birds.
Summer with all its hubbub.
If too much for you, get in the house
And wait for fall.

SCHOOL

Coast along, study what you like,
Skip what you dislike
That's bad.
'Cause you know it's coming. It's sad.
Sits in the back of your head
It's coiled and ready to spring.
As you look ahead.
Swim and play, hunt and fish
Laugh and play, doing fake downtime.
Without a single rhyme.
The fun is dispelled when the days arrive
You enter the room, your morose single file
Beads of worry all the while
Oh! I know why I disliked school
I disliked not knowing when to stop playing
And it's too late, it's presented. Final.

MEXICO

Why do I know of its beauty
Without having been there
I listened when I heard
Milder climates, someone said
Bright umbrella plants with different greens.
Beaches. Pristine. Beautiful beaches.
White sands. Hot.
And see for miles underwater.
Clear like glass with blaring mobile reds and aquas.
Language rich and romantic.
Rich foods delicious
And beautiful people. I've seen photos.
I'm going skiing in Mexico.

NEIGHBORS

Some are nice
Some are mean
Others are neutral
Not meaning anything
Some you don't know,
They wave and smile
I guess wishing you well
But really thinking I hope you fall in a well.
Does that mean I'm thinking
I hope they fall in a well
When I think they might be thinking
They hope I fall in a well?
I wonder
and wander

KNOW HOW TO FIX A BROKEN LEG

A doctor could do it better
But I could splint it secure for weeks
Without gangrene
Then remove it and the leg would be okay
To use again, to walk and run
Be harder, more brittle
To break easier next time
I know

THE LIZARD KING

I went walking down a long sidewalk
Along a street paved west
It was ten on a Friday, less shade for the road
The tar softening in the sun
A wooded area was right as I went west.
And a fence at its outlines with worn wooden slats
Near clumps of foliage at the fence corner
Was a paper cup
On passing I heard scratching about the cup
I'm reminded to check it on the way back
Later I spun and headed East.
Curious of the cryptic scratching
I brushed leaves back and looked inside.
A lizard it was
That made that scuttling noise
It was tiptoeing in this twelve-ounce container
Sloshing around some cold black coffee
Great, it hasn't been here long.
It still looked fierce, was lively and rotund.
I gently poured it out on a post.
It looked like a wood lizard, maybe an anole.
Still as a stork and glaring after one tilt.
Did it know I saved it from possible risk?
It darted. And was gone.
I really didn't see it leave
Back to its woods, into the mix.
Its instinctive balance it brings

ALARM CLOCK

The alarm clock mostly wakes
Me when I set it to.
Sometimes I wake up a minute before or two.
It has a snooze button
That I never use.
So, should I get an alarm clock
Without a snooze button?
And do they make those?
I really do worry too much.

MOWING THE LAWN

Make some squares.
Section it out.
Mow the squares for
Intermittent breaks
With water, tea, or beer
While admiring the turf.
Then do it again and again and
Again and again.
As grass grows fast.

AT THE LIBRARY

Sitting at the library typing up some words
Distracted by someone three chairs down
Coughing, gasping, sneezing, and breathing hard
Loudly clearing his throat, expressing a frown
Groaning and panting
Sounding almost like a dog
Leaving often through another door
To the bathroom, coughing more efficiently there
Earphones on, listening to something
I thought it was a joke at first
Then it stopped, he stood up and pointed up
And said it was dust in the AC ducts
He asked the two of us if we felt it too
We said not at all, you must be sick or have the flu
He said he had it in Iraq and Iran as well
We said had what, pray tell
The reply was pollen and dust was there too
I said these libraries are bad for you
The other patron agreed this was apparently true
We tersely saluted and thanked him for his bravery
It's unique people who fight in other countries
He finally collected his gear and left
Bidding us good day and to avoid the waft.

GIRLFRIEND

I had a girlfriend, years on and off.
I made her mad and she moved out
One apartment over
And we became closer.
I got a house.
She made it a home.
She wanted to be close to her parents,
Out of state.
I moved her.
After many months she said she wanted to be back.
I did not miss her yet and said,
"I heard you can still be soulmates even long distance."
She got mad and hung up.
Now I do miss her and cannot call her.
I talk with her parents.
They're out of the mix
And me not asking.
The funny thing is,
I really did hear of long-distance soulmates.

PENS

Ballpoint pens. You see them everywhere.
In venues for the taking,
I'm telling you. I'm not faking.
You grab one while on the phone.
I spied one while landing a drone.
While leaving the store they jump in your pocket,
Some dangle next to a locket.
A friend in a parking lot counted twenty-one.
I turned right, then left and stepped on one.
Buy them in ten packs, fifty packs, and more.
How much ink can these beaked squids pour?
Excuse me; I need to jot something down.
You got a pen on you?

RETIREMENT

Here's a plan
When it gets here I'll strive to exercise
While conserving energy
Needing less food, water, and beer
I'll drive not often, saving gas, wear-and tear
Keep the lights off, cut AC back
Open the windows and adjust to darker
Don't travel much, which I already do
Eat more fruit, deterring doctors,
Eat less, lose weight, get thin, get toned
Walk straighter, walk it faster
Better posture, healthy heart
I'll drink water instead of cola
Live longer and prothsper.

RELIGION

Isn't it manmade
Not created by God?
Then why go to church?
This is planet earth.
You can pray on the pot.
Good Lord, he doesn't care
Where you impress
When you're casting the best,
His words
To still hate to fight and
Keep faith and good
For humans and animals alike.

PONIES

I live in Texas and never rode a horse
I went to Virginia and rode a horse
Not very well
The horse knew this and tried to kill me.
It ran under low branches
Stopped abruptly in the water
It bucked and tried to roll
I held on. I was a fool.
Then it stood
I looked at this horse with its still strong will
A thousand riders none the same
I jumped off, gave it an apple and a hug
I felt strong for this horse
Its ears and eyes a voice
Said I have no choice who jumps on my back
With hundreds of riders I have to adapt
Light ones were tolerated, heavies were not
Dumb Estebans I fought a lot
What a challenge it had and way serious
It wanted only one rider to trust.

RAIN

Sometimes rain rain rain rain
Rain rain rain rain
And at times rain
And other times no rain and
No rain while needing rain
Often depending on time of year
And/or if the boy is here.

www.ingramcontent.com/pod-product-compliance
Lightning Source LLC
Chambersburg PA
CBHW070101260726

How to Overcome Anxiety, Stress and Panic Naturally

Set Aside Your Worries and Start Living

By: Steven Edwards

9781634289948

PUBLISHERS NOTES

Disclaimer – Speedy Publishing LLC

This publication is intended to provide helpful and informative material. It is not intended to diagnose, treat, cure, or prevent any health problem or condition, nor is intended to replace the advice of a physician. No action should be taken solely on the contents of this book. Always consult your physician or qualified health-care professional on any matters regarding your health and before adopting any suggestions in this book or drawing inferences from it.

The author and publisher specifically disclaim all responsibility for any liability, loss or risk, personal or otherwise, which is incurred as a consequence, directly or indirectly, from the use or application of any contents of this book.

Any and all product names referenced within this book are the trademarks of their respective owners. None of these owners have sponsored, authorized, endorsed, or approved this book.

Always read all information provided by the manufacturers' product labels before using their products. The author and publisher are not responsible for claims made by manufacturers.

This book was originally printed before 2014. This is an adapted reprint by Speedy Publishing LLC with newly updated content designed to help readers with much more accurate and timely information and data.

Speedy Publishing LLC

40 E Main Street, Newark, Delaware, 19711

Contact Us: 1-888-248-4521

Website: http://www.speedypublishing.co

REPRINTED Paperback Edition: ISBN: 9781634289948

Manufactured in the United States of America